SOMNIA
Maria Stadnicka

Newton-le-Willows

Published in the United Kingdom in 2020
by The Knives Forks And Spoons Press,
51 Pipit Avenue,
Newton-le-Willows,
Merseyside,
WA12 9RG.

ISBN 978-1-912211-50-0

Acknowledgements:

Early versions of these poems were published in: *Axon* (Australia), *Dissident Voice* (US), *International Times* (UK), *Ink, Sweat and Tears* (UK), *Litter* (UK), *Mary Evans Picture Library* (UK), *Meniscus* (Australia), *Molly Bloom* (UK), *Osiris* (US), *Social Alternatives* (Australia), *Stride* (UK), *Tears in the Fence* (UK), *Tenebrae* (UK), *The Poets' Republic* (UK), *The Journal* (UK), & *Shearsman Magazine* (UK).

A heartfelt thank you for all the generosity, support and guidance to Alan Baker, Ionut Boghian, Lesley Burt, Rosie Byrd, David Caddy, Carlie Chabot, Tom Costello, Tom Dwight, Anna Gosson, Beatrice Hitchman, Adam Horovitz, Peter J. King, Jack Little, Morag Kiziewicz, Mark Mawer, Katie McCue, Hugh McMillan, Andrea Morehead, Adelaide Morris, Andrew Morrison, Alec Newman, Stuart Paterson, Hayley Porri, Jay Ramsay, Philip Rush, Hayley Saunders, Aidan Semmens, Steve Spence, John Stadnicki, Natalina Stadnicki, Rick Vick, Samuel de Weer, Jen Whiskerd, Jane Woodend and Neil Young.

Warmest gratitude for the invaluable editorial suggestions and belief in my work to Rupert Loydell, as well as Angela France and Nigel McLoughlin.

Supported using public funding by

ARTS COUNCIL ENGLAND

LOTTERY FUNDED

Contents

Movement III: Scherzo

Movement IV: Finale

Epilogue

SOMNIA

(Four Movements in F Minor)

to Cain and Abel, and all their neighbours

'You can get a lot done with a bayonet,
but sitting on one is uncomfortable.'

– Svetlana Alexievich

Prologue

Your Honour, this is the truth.
On rare occasions, I look back
and all I remember is
the start of a story
about
a king whose left eye smiled
every time he looked in the mirror;
his right eye wept every time he saw
a different man gazing back at him through glass.

Movement I: Allegro

'The bomb will explode in the bar at twenty past one. Now it's only sixteen minutes past. Some will still have time to enter, some to leave.'

– Wislawa Symborska

Sonata

It starts in broad daylight
with a study in curves,

with pencils,
sharpened by schoolboys,
over many hours of labour,
building-building a vessel
just before she hissed
I shall pray for you.

I laugh, turn the machine off,
move closer to anger:
hands, metal, ankles, metal, eye.
Metal! Nerves.

We practise human squares
and circles,
indifferent to losing
something irreplaceable.

North

Imagine we are in a train crossing the Urals,
leaning against the back door, watching
spirals of barbed wire spike up towards light.

Further, inland, somebody looking like you
climbs up the mountains' vertical. On his back,
a box the size of your ribcage.

Inside the chest, a trapped bird reaches forward;
her hours, frozen water droplets, lined up on ribbons.

Our foreheads face North. Through glass,
the landscape speeds away. Ears listen to knocks
coming from a different compartment;
our fingertips touch cold feathers in mid-flight.

The train suddenly stops and the man looks back,
dropping the cube into abyss. Faint sounds echo in circles.
Smaller and smaller.

Far out here, we put our eyes to the bird's eye
and come out running.

Witness

At the supermarket's meat counter,
they sell ropes. Yellow and blue. Things
we need when weather turns bad.
One could never be sure when the boat
needs tying off to a cleat.
At checkout, we talk of hurricane Ursula.
It was in the news, it is now by the docks.
My bottled green sea is resting on shelves.

Across the aisle, a woman looks out.
Trains deliver milk and morning newspapers;
at the end of his shift, a night watchman
lights a cigarette watching umbrellas running
to shelter. He has nowhere else. His children
sent him a blank telegram. *Monochrome winds,*
he thinks. *Time to repair, to build.*
The house he was born in no longer exists.

Landscape with Knives

A busy Saturday at the market.
Hunger wears friendly nametags.
A miracle healer pale as milk
passes by selling dream-crumbs.

His voice trapped between
tall cement granite marble.
Blessed be these bullets;
many have dropped over us.

At the Post Office, queues move
through smoke pillars;
hot earth lifted above treelines.

Two burning men run towards water;
between them, a cracked stone
watches red-purple clouds.

Fireballs spark downwards,
at dawn, windows are shut.

Words lock themselves in silvery knots
just before they become people.
We take turns at remembering: sleep,
days before ash, a ringing doorbell.

Screams bite rooftops.
The knives have woken up
to meet chopping boards.

Shooting Position

We queue at the airport,
pretending to watch
a lunar eclipse.

We fear sharp objects.
Passengers hold boarding passes up,
flags in a moving crusade.

All windows are half-open,
but nobody looks out.
Heat seals glossy layers
of mist over my homeland.

We have outgrown the raincoat
tripping over someone's thoughts
in the two-minute stop between stations.

At odd times, the planes take off.
Letters drop from above
on neighbouring gardens,

seeds growing tall in silent parks.
We remove luggage tags, barely notice
the music of a mid-air explosion.

Blades of grass stand ready to shoot.

Traffic

It is the longest day
and the sun swerves left-right left-right,
hits pedestrians watching a bullfight.

On the opposite lane,
a runner in standby, reading *Nausea*;
his baby wails in a pram chewing a rifle.

From a distance the gun fires at us:

The bullet hits the edge of my book
then sinks into earth like a poem
dropped from a bridge.

Urban rumours carry on forward,
indicating an obstacle in the road.
Childless vehicles, late for work.

Nobody looks ahead.
Nobody looks behind.
My shadow jumps on a live grenade.

The city empties.

Karenin

not long after doctors decide to stop treatment,
I feel hair locks growing inside my lungs

/a footnote, not headline/

asphyxia, earthquake, someone younger
lost at sea pushes his way out through my vocal cords;

poison, drowning, mute wedding photo watches
from the bedside table in my hospital room;

at this point, John Coltrane appears on stage
to play 'Giant Steps' as a nurse breaks free

from the audience she asks me to sign
a disclosure agreement before turning off
life support

/falling, the hydrogen bomb does not have
time to ask the victims of their age/

the day closes, enters the geometric kingdom:
ctrl alt delete

Morphology

It is said that a body remembers
what the soldier would not:

indoors' neat captivity
reflected in shuttered mirrors,
bullet's hiding corner,
the memory of violent love
and other word combinations
one comes across between layers of flesh.

With each breath, the bones take turns
at forgetting the knockout mechanism.

State of Execution

It simply dawns on me.
The minute I touch
her memory,
a fortress collapses.

blood gushes out for shelter

Death does not talk.
She pulls my trousers up,
she hides me under a stone.

Landscape with Buses

On both sides of the frontline,
orchards in bloom.
People buy and sell goods,
occupy central squares,
dogs run after barefoot children
with grain baskets – linen flags.
Buses on schedule, taxis in queue.

Business as usual.
Gunshots, grenades, mortars.

Stray barks come out of houses
with blown-up windows. Splinters
rising – morning's canines.
Soldiers wake up to the call to prayer,
switch radio on, shave by the roadside.
Nametags rest in shoe polish tins,
heat bakes bread already sliced.
Buses carry wounded further inland.

Punctus Contra Punctum

From time to time, we stand
between a wolf and a dog,

germinate inside tight handbags
falling into a moment of muteness.

We are expected to root,
given the choice of death.

A step closer, a level higher
in a battery-operated game:

nobody comes in
without prior agreement.

The recoiled bow springs out
unleashed howl.

At a steady pace
we catch a moving train.

Movement II: Largo

'Wait! You! Your name's is not here, I don't see it.'

– Anna Akhmatova

Spring Cleaning

Tuesday with dust shining on jars
and Clara piles memories in black bags.
Cleaning day she says.

Up and down the stairs, one-winged sister
trips over my legs, keeps singing,
the tune slides across walls, butterflies jump
from her mouth on her head then out.

I wonder what butterfly meat tastes like,
if sliced with a silver blade; what mother tasted like
the moment she released me – honey coated pearl.
I smell the skin on my wrists: mother's hiding place.

The day she left to buy bread I tell Clara,
she had stilettos, a hat, mid-eighties permed hair;
grown long to her ankles by now.

. . . she sets fire to old carpets,
fibres curl, briefly spark, die off in smoke.
Our dolls rest on rubbish bin's lid.
The house fills up with mid-eighties permed ashes.

Playground

I

On the way home, we walk
through a building site
with half-bricked houses. My shadow
    hops alongside his, fireflies
    light up the top of a church.

Look, the clouds, like a girl playing
mummy and daddy between metal cranes;
she hums lullabies, her dolls float in the sky.
Let's take her with us. She's barefoot.

Father hurries ahead. His boots
drag the field's mud. His work-tools
    in a satchel over my shoulder.
Let's bloody leave it and go, he says.

Let's climb up and give her some fudge;
she might be hungry.

Father hurries ahead: *Come along, dog, it's dark.*

II

The circus is here, the circus is here,
look, two caged lions fighting each other:
fangs bite below knee, claws hook fur tears,
blood spatters rise, dust all over us.

Behind curtains, a buffoon in uniform,
folding arms across his chest, looks up.
Red seconds complete full circle,
an acrobat stumbles between bars.

It's the interval. The magician wakes up
half-dreaming he found sodium hydroxide.

Spotlights flicker, a tightrope walker
points at us to join in the middle as
a skinny horse crawls onstage,
barely breathing, stomach ripped open.

We ran to play, gently peeling its skin.
Underneath, flesh clings to its frame.

The audience is cheering.
People laugh, blowing bubbles
as we laugh *Kill or be killed*.
The show is fantastic.

III

They ask me to eat earth
and kneel on the grass. I bite my tongue
as the soil talks back in our language.

I show them how the tar makes
the best chewing-gum when picked
off the pavement after a heatwave.

Our mirror reflects the sun into the headlights
of speeding cars; the drivers' faces light up
like overexposed photographs.

The first to snap a bird's neck
gets a lollipop from Father Michael.
My hands flutter, the wings
knot around my wrist.

I hold my breath. We give it a burial
behind the Laundry Block. One of us
swings Father's censer over the grave.

My fist up to my face whistles
all things bright. Across the garden, a robin
watches the myrrh burning to ashes.

Defence Mechanism

Would you kill a bird?
The angel stops to light
a cigarette and says
nothing back.

The silence throbs
in my fist, as I move
rubble pieces
across the chess table
unsure what bishops,
rooks, pawns are for
in this game.

Would you kill a bird?
the angel asks me.
A stone grows
in my mouth.
Between my flesh
and my heart,

        rust.

Siege

I sit up and hear crowds
above the laundry lines.

Another boat must have capsized
and the souls tried to escape
through a recently painted door.

On the island, rifles at round-up.
The young are shot first
in pitch black, it takes a while
to clean up the streets.

Fishing nets return empty.
Mothers' tangled hair gets caught
in a fight with waves bigger than them.

A soldier walks through an alleyway,
singing, knocks over an empty milk bottle.

I go back to sleep holding tight on to a lost rubber doll.

Bolshoi Rehearsal

53.2. Numbers blink, red dots on scales
show my thighs have grown
by two-hundred grams. I open the window.
Adverts for dance productions hang across skies,
a heavy woman squeezes against glass
to make room for me.

For lunch, I swallow crushed ice,
wood shavings, a full glass of tap water;
jump on the treadmill: thirty-eight minutes,
three-point-two miles, three hundred calories.
Lost two-hundred grams.

A neighbour rings, invites me to dinner
saying the man living at number four died,
hit by a bus on the way to the gym.
He was 73 kilos. I am 53.

I stop eating protein, google public transport
routes, pick-up times for stones-pounds.
Every day at 9:45, a stout driver reminds passengers:
No hot food at the back. Only light snacks.

Indoors. Drawing jogging maps
on steaming shower curtains.
Shampoo waves on my striped ribcage.
Sea splashes away in the bathroom.
Sand grains hide in my shoe.

Chair in the Audience

I am nobody. A blind pigeon
jumps up on roofs.
Click-clack! Click-clack!
The summer ends.

On the landing, a letter for me;
its heartbeat stares into space
through the unsealed envelope.

I have no followers.
I follow no one.
I eat the supper in silence,
polish my armour.
Click-clack! Click-clack!

My beak touches ground.

M5

After a power cut, waterlogged hours
unravel dimming dark threads.

The motorway's in standstill.

A wonder-bird drives past
the Suspension Bridge,
leaving the nest to defend itself.

Sleet gets through her dress,
gropes her heart's corner.

Roadworks keep the candlelight going
for sleepy men digging out earth;
mother-wings fly off
towards something uncertain.

Here, distance is all that matters,
before the absolute stop.

A stranger at the steering wheel, in free fall.

Headline

Late at night, the sidewinds push the car
off the road. They make an emergency stop.

No city in sight, nor visible lights. They
cannot see a landmark in the rear-view mirror.
Just absence and floods.

Between treetops, one of them spots
a planet hanging down, tilted off balance
and gets closer to look at its shadow.

The further he travels, the deeper the quicksand.
The earth sobs, shooting star comes to life,
he steps out of view.

Nobody Saw, Nobody Heard

On Easter Sunday, father goes missing.
I find the bakery door wide open,
and the loaves burning to ashes; the wireless
crushed. Glass, oil, grains on the mud floor,
and the salt jar smashed against the back wall.

State your name for the record.
My name is Marcus Aurelius.

I look everywhere for him.
In the yard and the local bodega.
Up the hill, at the cemetery.
I ask the neighbours.
Nobody saw, nobody heard.

Citizen Aurelius, we have brought
the evidence against your name.

He returns home after a week with the shirt
he is wearing covered in blood. His hair
has turned white. He can barely see me,
says he lost his glasses in the KGB basement.
He never speaks again after this.

Cartagena
to Rupert Loydell

When I collected my father's ashes
at the crematorium
I thought to keep them hidden
in a pencil case.

The undertaker handed back
his old beer-stained passport
and postcards from cities
he had planned to visit one day.

That night, in my hotel,
I fell asleep in his clothes, dreamt
a room filled with journeys and ink.
Smoky seeds ready for new soil.

Father's hand moved across maps
and pointed the Danube, the Volga,
the sea with its blackness.
I jumped awoken by rain on a wet deck.

Woman Walking

I always wanted mother's nightdress,
hoped she would leave it to me;
the flowery cotton she wore on Saturdays
when she carried yellow baskets of laundry
out to the garden's well. Our nights
followed her around; washed, starched,
pegged rainbows on silver wires.
The street inhaled jasmine-fresh clouds.

I wanted blue shadowed eyelids,
shiny stilettos down Pushkin Avenue
when she hurried back home from the office
with doughnuts kept warm at her breast.
And to wear adulthood just like that:
battle decoration pinned on yellow dress.

When last we spoke, she looked away;
she'd forgotten what yellow meant,
put a finger inside curled petals to feel heat.
A foreign woman in black walked on cobwebs,
calling my name. The moon grew larger
and trees split, struck by an axe of frost.
Mother went silent – maybe she fell asleep –
and her nightdress turned into snow.

Noise

I had a poetry reading at the passage
under the M5, between junctions 12 and 13.
Hurried people listened on chairs,
watching the highway talk in verse
when a coughing fit made me weep,
see past exhaust pipes the roads leading
straight to theirs hearts – precise lanes
on satellite navigation systems.
Nobody cried, nobody laughed.
Winter holiday arrived with fireworks
when they stood up and left.
Roadside lights switched off behind them.

Objects

tomorrow lived in this house
yellow-red bursts heated
     mute water pipes

afternoons passed lettering names

we exchanged poems for shoes
we'd bought at the market

we had no written instructions
for *happy* until a bailiff came
to collect your dresses and scarves

I gently obliged   made tea

tomorrow left us the walls
        of right-here-right-now

Dear Sir,

a beauty company sent me an email,
We win, you win, it said, invited me
to purchase youth serum at half price.

There is something I hate about emails
sitting like this – urgent black on screen:
comma after verb, mistaken for breath
taken when reading poems aloud.

Please, do not reply, it carried on
we hope to see you again.
I rush to the bathroom to see
how deep my forehead lines
have grown since I last checked.

Skin tracks' network shows
how much I've won in forty years
of living too small, dreaming too big.

Particulars

I went out to town and took pictures
of people in queue at the shopping mall.
A third of them had been there since Friday;
pilgrims and parents in search of new praying beads.

They sat on the pavement holding
their thoughts between knees. The sun
kept quiet in its corner and watched
the autumn busking outdoors
when a beggar stopped, asking everyone
for directions to the nearest abattoir.

Nobody knew precisely where the roads led,
but smiled back through the surveillance cameras.

Dusk

You climb up the stairs with a folded newspaper.
I already know tomorrow's news from feeds
and hashtags, having spent an entire day, enjoying
a virtual feast. I haven't got time to be here
but I have dreams written on torn flags.

My present clutters with fragments of past
which do not fit the puzzle. Your slipper calls
for help from the landing. I respond and follow
you up to bed. I stand beside my older self
with the same grace mother lay in her coffin.

Poetics

I had a disagreement with a poetry master
about wolves. And talking made me think
that I, too, had the same great fear
of words living forever, but said nothing.

I watched birds flying at low altitude,
tongue knotted twisting commas,
and full stops came out of my mouth;
it hurt as badly as losing a war.

The poet walked away, locked himself
in a room with many doors but no handles.
Outside, his tamed wolf sat guarding the exits.

Mine wanted to jump from a cloud
straight into the blank page.
A child passed by and said
wolves don't exist on paper. Only in flesh.

Movement III: Scherzo

'I was, I am or I shall be a question of grammar and not of existence.'

– Emil Cioran

Habitatum

I live at the top floor,
in a flat with a view
to a perfect car park.

I take white little stones
and place them, like pills,
in straight lines on my desk.

Through a hole in the sky,
I watch the beheadings
going on in the city
and point a fully-loaded gun
against the world.

My earth rests, suspended
between wild heavens
and landscaped gardens.

The sun hangs loose
above silent bell ropes
as if nothing has happened.

Press Release

I used to know a man who lived in a windmill.
He had the habit of finishing off people's thoughts.

He kept leaving water glasses at a junction
where the elm tree, he used to know,
had been suddenly cut down.

In December, he painted the ceiling
a red-evening sky, saying it did not hurt
when something you love gets replaced by a shadow.

He was in the paper for a head-punch he'd given
to a new-born puppy.

When he died, they found
a breathing child tucked in his breast pocket.

The Soloist

So sorry. The doctor delivered
the bad news one morning.
Life, I gather, is full of surprises.

I could smell skin as he talked,
so fast, I don't remember
any of the words except his tie.

I looked around, saw
he'd left the room
and set off across a field.

Arriving home, I noticed
how quiet the streets were.

In my flat, life carried on,
protected by wolves.

Composition

After a hot day, a midnight siren
startled Igor Stravinsky.

Whenever he heard anyone speaking
he rushed to the door

with a brush or something more permanent
he left shaky marks on the wall.

One, two, only four people passed by,
satellites tracked the time it took him to blink.

By morning, all that silence
worked its way back into a cello.

Zoom

In the back of a car,
a thought held his hand,
adjusted his glasses

did I die in a crash?
or maybe they waved
from a bedroom window

the words multiplied,
the ropes played with children
but none of us

had the courage
to move closer
for fear of making too much noise.

He had recently taken up chess.
When the bullet hit, he was
planning the next move.

Between two windowpanes
a shortcut to heaven. That
mid-giggle blast, rotating

stuck in familiar music box
stood out flour trace
leading us to the crime scene.

Out of the cinema,
the crowd felt the slaughter
and rushed to unsee, unhear.

The blinds were drawn.
The camera zoomed in.
The lullaby malfunctioned.

Mundane Evil

There was a wake going on
in a floor crack. So much old wood
talked back in mother's tongue
through the opening that I thought
to wait longer for the right moment
and then a close friend pointed out
the rupture took shape, got wider.
My womb coughed out pieces of rubble.

Kafka

The other day, during an afternoon nap,
a tramp came to my door with a letter
for the man in apartment three, ground floor.

The knock made me jump, then I thought
I could give out some change in return,
but the beggar refused; he was holding
a bunch of keys and left saying *'till tomorrow.*

When I opened the envelope, lying flat
in my bunk, a pair of handcuffs and
steel neck chains dropped on my chest.

Lieder for Two Pianos
to Clara and Luca

At first, I counted heartbeats,
checked for sudden changes
in atmospheric pressure
when something told me
you slept too close to water.

Your cries squeezed
the cords of my flesh
until milk-tears would burst.
The primal hunger kept us awake.

With time, I started saving
my last mouthful,
half-swallowed lullabies found you
growing hazel-eyed whispers inside my body.
In crowds, I walked ahead,
my palms sheltered your dreams.

The waters came one night
and touched your back.
The candle's tip turned off
the promise *I'll keep you safe* …
Time knew you'd leave by morning.

Point Blank

At the end of each day,
you climb into bed
and cover your face.
Our bodies fuse,
resemble an owl
trapped under floorboards.

Somewhere out in the world
bells ring announcing a burial
but the gravedigger's already left.

Summer is taking over;
meadows expand
beyond our reach. Too late now.

Visiting Hours

I

they no longer
drink tea, listen, squeeze swearwords;
at the top floor, they see
a paper-girl trying on black dresses,
her teeth bite the blue
through a window left open

> life rolls over me
> like a nurse, close to my bed,
> handing me a visiting ticket;
> I collar her, state I am
> not through yet

II

they cover orange candle holders
and climb ladders

> my loose living-room socks
> hang, still warm, around my neck
> tic-tac! tic-tac!

III

they whisper and nibble and cough
the silence crumbles
the cars move in the same direction

> trapped without oxygen mask
> I'm well-dressed to watch
> my funeral going ahead

Movement IV: Finale

'. . . my last wish was that there should be a crowd of spectators at my execution and that they should greet me with cries of hatred.'

– Albert Camus

Eyelids

Everyone said they were looking
in the opposite direction
when the car hit.

The sun, high, covered the scene with blankets.
The coins dropped on their eyelids.
The traffic stopped.

We went closer to watch.
For some time,
unreturned phone calls echoed in dust.

Puppetry

One evening, at a dinner party, we hear
the Puppet Master telling his guests
that the laws of supply and demand
do not apply to us. We look well,
happy in the fuzzy video footage
he uploaded online; we do not mind
waiting for our turn in his bunker.

In the ballroom upstairs,
the sky returns to its normal grey.
In the basement, we keep busy talking
about far-away soldiers on night patrol.

A guest says to another *Nothing clears
the remains of the war better than
a new haircut.* We are dutiful dolls
as the Puppet Master cuts off our curls.
When he flings the door open to let us out,
the world unfolds in rows of empty spaces.

Luggage

This morning a revolution begins
with a fight between my sister and I
over a plate of stale breadcrumbs.

News in the background: no school today;
a bomb exploded on our playground
and reporters interview the war hero.
Then a short weather forecast:
bleak, minus, Western chill.

Silence follows the samovar's whisper,
our small hands finish homework.
Arched backs break bearing too many words –
heavy crumbs fall between eyelashes.

Father sips boiled leaves, watching
Dynamo Kiev versus Beshiktash,
live on TV, in Champions League. Nil-nil.
Offside, free kick, foul. Crowds wave
half-burnt flags, defenceless against
the penalty shot: the ball flies
West-East and hits the bar.

Outside kitchen window,
orphan trees march towards distant borders.
We do not lift our eyes from the page,
do not see anything but ourselves,
packing maps, colours, memories –
essentials for a world on foot.

In my satchel, baking paper wraps up
the infinite possibilities of one-way roads.

Live Show

A dog wakes up at dawn
to finish his homework,

his softly spoken brother
makes tea, laughs at

the passing postman
who trips over a stone.

An owl gets home
from a night shift, critical

of the morning noise:
boiling water setting a fire alarm.

The sun looks back
forgets where to go next

the radio airs an interview
with a PR consultant.

He answers all the questions
with *yes*. The ground swells.

Transcript

When the truth eventually came out
they said all the vital preparations were made.

Something essential stopped them half-way.
Late, almost there, almost present.

If they had waited a bit longer,
someone would have noticed
the sudden passing of a short miracle.

The Gift's Legacy
to Nikesh Shukla

To be migrant in the twenty-first century
and be offered a gift, which refused
turns into weapon against the well-wisher;

to be migrant in waiting;
        remember that time, at the cinema …
        we went to watch horror movies
        in an empty auditorium …
        terrified of the dark
        but kept wide-eyed at the screen,
        until a man put the lights on,
        reminding us we had stayed there a whole day;

to become responsible
for a bullet wound, though we have
no memory of ever using a gun,
in the name of each person wishing to be free.

Fruit Season

Tomorrow has rain written on banners
stretched far-yellow and further-blue.

Where we sit, language tastes of meat,
of cubes on neck-throat-tongue
in a process of decompression.

It has the chill of piled-high books
fertilising an orchard in bud;
bitterness floods her rope.

During the fruit season, men,
far too strong, spit out unearthed chapters.
Tomorrow's country births paper colonies.

Time measures in icy ground marks.
Hollow seed reaches our wide-open mouths.

Nervous Twitch

All year long, we drink from the same well.
We hold the clay with both hands
waiting for people to accept their fate.

We begin with the words *we are*,
watching blood's linger on roads and hotels,
on and off, praying in opposite changing-rooms.
We know why things happen differently
than how we'd imagined at school, over red-eyed desks.

Everything we build lives inside lungs
taken out of a ripped-up beast.

Frost

We have waited so long to speak
that now face to face
we taste the garden pebble
secretly growing older.

        None of us had news
from Guantánamo – but then
there are never any missives
once the frost settles in.

Somnia

When the executioner's bored
he turns dangerous.
Tapping noises sweep his room
and chill streams up from the ground.

He reaches between bars
picking up a blood-stained prayer book;
keeps reading the psalms, falling asleep
with his back against a sharp blade.

Morning comes
and a sword sprouts out of his spine.

Inheritance

I thread cotton fibres in a factory
on the outskirts. The looms' dust settles
inside my lungs, the iron bites, and rust
grows tangled over my heart.

Beyond the city, my children's eyes
are dimming; their restless glow
switches off in a long, narrow dorm.
Orphans but free, the cloth says
then keeps talking to me
about the people I once loved,
who vanished during a blast
as if they had never existed.

The houses, pulled apart, inherit
my flesh and my ruins. Unhealed
wounds weaving the fabric of tears.
These hands church vestments
as the city gives birth to a prophet.

Poetics
to Nichita Stanescu

The soldier, like a poet, awaits
the start of her fight, waving
at people she does not know.
They remind her of home.
Once they all go to sleep,
she measures and trims
the infinite distance between
rooms concealed in her heart.

The poet, like a soldier, does
not have rooms. Her heart bears
its own weight, her story
is smithereens and smoke.
The poet would sleep anywhere
just to be in the same town
with you. She does not have
her own place in the world yet.

Journal Page

We inhabit the world's pipeline,
picking up fallen apples. Friends
who died of battlefield injuries
turn into slow burning paragraphs.

We inhabit churches and prayers
floating from cell to cell,
and damp kisses: our proofs
that we remain enemies.

Beneath the viewpoint, air currents
force tired birds into submission.
From our enclosure we like watching
them fall, talking about ourselves,

pretending to see the whole
in small incisions below the continuum.
In truth, knowing too much about
the ferocious nature of man.

Epilogue

Your Honour, it's closing time.
The coat is over my shoulder.
In hurry to exit, I long to know
how it ends on the last page,
afraid of being unworthy
of my suffering.

Lightning Source UK Ltd.
Milton Keynes UK
UKHW012338250620
365566UK00005B/913